A 31-DAY DEVOTIONAL

Girl Get Up! A 31-Day Devotional
Copyright ©2023 by Stacy Hyman
ISBN: 9789768304315

Unless otherwise noted, all scripture quotations are from the New King James Version of the Bible. Copyright © 1982 by Thomas Nelson, Inc. Used by permission. All rights reserved.

Scripture quotations taken from the 21st Century King James Version®, copyright © 1994. Used by permission of Deuel Enterprises, Inc., Gary, SD 57237. All rights reserved.

Cover Photo: by Cglade from Getty Images Signature
Cover & Interior font: www.canva.com

Interior Design & Layout: Shelev Publishing
Email: Shelevpublishing@outlook.com
Instagram: ShelevPublishing
Facebook: ShelevPublishing
Telephone: 1 (246) 257-9611

Dedication

Movies and cartoons have painted pictures of what angels should look like. Long flowing hair, glowing and radiating glory, but I've never seen such an angel. Instead, I had one who walked and talked with me.

When I was a little girl, I used to clean the neighbor's fridge and receive a little cash in return. She then told her friend who lived close to us about me, and I cleaned her fridge as well. Eulene was her name, but I called her Richie. She was not one to allow many people in her house, but somehow, she liked me. I was quite a rebellious young girl, which made the relationship with my mom difficult, so I would often go by Richie to get away from it all. One look at me and Richie would know when something was up.

We built such a strong relationship that I even started telling her I was her adopted daughter. Everyone knew I was her little girl. Richie was a listening ear, someone I could confide in. She would always encourage and feed me continuously. I love food. Lol. Her family was also loving and kind to me. Even as I got older, I was still the little girl from down the road to her. Who knew that cleaning her fridge would lead to such a beautiful friendship? God really knows how to connect us with the right people to nurture us. I met an angel in human form who touched my life. A stranger who became my family and buddy. She always thought I was a blessing to her, but as I reflect on my life, she was more of a blessing to me.

Richie is no longer here in body, but I carry her in my heart every single day, often reminiscing about the many jokes she would tell. She would always ask, "Stacy, you could stir Cou-Cou?" She never got over me telling her no. Richie, you are missed dearly by those who knew and loved you. I love you and I am grateful to have had you as a friend. I miss your laughs, your insults about my hair, and our movie nights.

I cannot imagine living life again without you. That would be pointless.

Acknowledgements

As a young girl growing up, my grandparents, my mother, and relatives always instilled gratitude. Simple words like "Thank you" and other kind gestures. Therefore, it is necessary that I acknowledge those who have made this book a success.

First, I give honor to Almighty God for choosing me even when I didn't choose myself. For His grace that saved and kept me and continues to help me get up when I fall.

I bless God for my hard-working mother, Faye. Mummy, I thank God that you kept me against all odds and brought me into this world. I only pray to be half as strong of a woman as you are and to make you proud. Your labor has not gone in vain. When they said, "Send them back to Guyana." You kept us beside you and raised us. I love you.

I give honor to my pastors, Apostle Rudder & Rev. Rudder for encouraging me to pursue this gift that God has given me. Your spiritual leadership has played a pivotal role in the woman I am and still becoming. For that, I thank you both.

I thank God for my former secondary school Daryll Jordan Secondary, and my past teachers who encouraged and helped me on my journey. It was there that God showed me it's not about where you go, but what you do when you get there.

To my inner circle Jewel, Davon and Akiem. I thank God for you three being by and on my side. Thank you for never shutting me down, for hearing my broken cries, and for seeing my wings even when I didn't.

To my beloved sister Vanessa, I bless God for the woman you are. I am grateful for every day that we are here together on this earth. We have accomplished and overcome a lot together by the power of God. Many think the strongest thing between us is our resemblance, but truly, it is our love for each other.

To my older siblings Ojay, Tracey and Terry. Thank you for being there and helping mummy to raise us. I love you all dearly.

To the friends I'm yet to meet, we have much to learn together; I await when our journey begins.

Dear Queen,

I wish I could give you a big, warm embrace. The sweetest hug that would touch that broken little girl on the inside. This journey of self-forgiveness doesn't happen in a day. Somehow, forgiving yourself isn't as easy as forgiving others. Yes, you have made some bad choices, but don't let that define who you are. The road to healing doesn't get easier, but you get stronger, and that makes it easier. You will cry many times, and if you're like my friend Shannon, whom I love dearly, you will cry tears and snot. Some days you will feel strong and other days extremely weak. Some days, you will beg God to make you forget the past and pray it never happened.

I want you to look at yourself in the mirror and embrace who you are about to become. Don't let people define you by your mistakes. Your worth is determined by who God says you are. The fact that you are still alive and reading this letter tells me you still have a lot of fight left in you! You are a warrior. What you have endured was meant to break you, but it built you instead.

You've been bound for too long. You've been lost for too long. You've been broken for too long. You've been laid back for too long. You've been running from your calling for too long! You've mourned the mistakes of your past long enough. You've cried enough over spilled milk. It is time to wipe your tears, forgive yourself, and move forward.

I am here to ignite that fire within you. To stir the gifts God has planted within you. I declare you will smile, love, and laugh again. You will cry tears of joy instead of tears of pain. By the power of the Holy Ghost, you are coming out! You are getting up from the rut and your story will be told, your voice will be heard.

God's plan for your life is far greater than any mistake you've made or will make. He can turn anything around for His honor and His glory. Girl Get Up, you've got big things to do!

-Love Stacy

Contents

Introduction

I've faced many trials and dealt with the repercussions of my choices. I followed my heart, which I shouldn't have, because as we know the Bible says the heart is deceitful above all else. I didn't adhere to counsel or obey God's voice; I was just about doing my thing. I eventually got to where I didn't feel like I could get up from my rut even though I knew God was calling me to do better. I recall trying to fight and move from that place, but every time I fought to get out, it was as though something would knock me back down.

I eventually gave up and became someone I didn't even know. Battling mentally, emotionally, physically, and spiritually. I lost a lot of weight and cried daily. It was as though my mistakes had become my identity. I knew I had lost myself, but I didn't know how to get her back. I knew I was struggling and searching, but I didn't know how to rebuild my relationship with God.

I remember one day being in the shower and hearing God say, "Girl Get Up." It was then I realized I needed to move from that place of hopelessness. It didn't mean that everything would be perfect, or I wouldn't fall again. But it was a decision I had to make and stick with. A decision to get up every single day and fight despite the troubling situations. I've had to forgive, heal and let go of things and let God be in control. A question usually asked is, "If you could go back, what would you change". There's a lot I could change, but I wouldn't have the lessons I have today.

My goal for this book is to help women get up and maximize their full potential in God. To help them understand, God can bring them back from anything. To encourage women to recover from the tragedies of life and choose to rise above whatever may come.

As you know, the healing process isn't always pretty, so your journey won't be one of perfection. You will encounter brokenness, make mistakes along the way, require forgiveness, and much more. But you know what? You will make it. God wants to perform open heart surgery on you so you can walk in purpose. He wants to pull some things out and replace them with joy, peace, love, goodness, and healing.

When you feel as though you can't go any further, you can always tag team God. He will be your strength. May this book be the arrow that shoots you forward into purpose, destiny and greatness. Sis, be encouraged in your heart and in your spirit. It's time to get up!

Part 1
Getting Up!

1

The Blame Game

"Then said Martha unto Jesus Lord, if thou hadst been here, my brother had not died". **John 11:21 KJV**

The first thing one must do in getting up from a spiritual rut is to stop playing the blame game. In John 11, news had reached Jesus that Lazarus, His friend, was dead. With this information, one would expect Jesus to drop everything to go see about his friend. Instead, the Bible tells us that Jesus stayed where He was two more days. Can you imagine that? When Jesus finally came, Martha cried out, "Lord, had you been here my brother would not have died." She had expected Jesus to come through for their family. After all, He was their friend. Martha's response was common. It came from a place of grief and sorrow over the loss of her brother. Many times, when we are going through trials, we do the same. We try to find someone to blame.

There was purpose in Lazarus' death and similarly in our lives. Everything we face serves a purpose. There is even purpose in death. For example, in order for us to have eternal life, Jesus had to be crucified. Lazarus's death was painful, but there was also purpose in it. Jesus raising Lazarus from the dead displayed His power over sin, death, and the grave. It showed that we who die in Christ will also be raised to eternal life.

Maybe you are going through a painful season right now and your entire world is falling apart. Everything looks like chaos and is changing faster than you can adjust. You have endured so much that some days you just don't have the strength. But you know what? It won't break you; it will build you.

What is your response when Jesus doesn't come through when you want? Are you like Martha? Ready to play the blame game? Whatever painful situation you have been going through, be encouraged. There is purpose in the pain. Give Jesus your pain and watch Him use it to bring glory to His name. Jesus knew Lazarus's ending, and He knows yours. So instead of looking for someone or something to blame, focus on drawing closer to the God, because He is the one who will bring you out on top.

Reflection

Are you currently blaming someone/something for a situation you are going through? Circle **YES/NO.** If yes, why are you blaming them?

_____

_____

_____

_____

_____

_____

_____

_____

_____

_____

_____

_____

_____

_____

Ask yourself if putting the blame on someone/something is of benefit to your healing process. Will it change anything?

2

Taking Responsibility

"Against thee, only thee. Have I sinned and done this evil in thy sight. That thou mightest be justified when thou speakest and be clear when though judgest".
Psalm 51:4 KJV

It's easy to blame others for the way our lives turn out. However, as we mature and become more self-aware, we must take responsibility for the role we play in our own suffering. The Psalmist David humbly came to realize that He had sinned against God. He could see that the choices he made played a major role in the destructive path he traveled.

Then David arose from the earth, and washed, and anointed himself, and changed his apparel, and came into the house of the Lord, and worshipped: then he came to his own house; and when he required, they set bread before him, and he did eat. **2 Samuel 12:20**

David's son he conceived with Bathsheba through adultery was sick. So, he fasted and prayed in sackcloth and ashes, hoping the Lord would relent and the child would live. Though he did all he could, his son died after seven days.

When he perceived the child was dead, he got up, washed and anointed himself, changed his clothes, and went to the house of the Lord to worship. He knew his actions had consequences, and there was nothing more he could do.

Sadly, there are many people who are still laying in sackcloth and ashes. Rather than humble themselves, repent and turn to Jesus, they are still covered in ashes of agony. Don't let this be you. It is time to take responsibility. We can all learn from the psalmist David and acknowledge our error and repent before God. At some point, we must take responsibility for the parts we play in our own suffering. It is honestly the only way we can move forward. We forgive, take responsibility for our actions, and turn to God.

Reflection

Are you ready to take responsibility? Circle **YES/NO.** If no, then why?

What does taking responsibility look like to you?

3

Returning Home

"And when he came to himself, he said, How many hired servants of my father's have bread enough and to spare, and I perish with hunger! I will arise and go to my father, and will say unto him, Father, I have sinned against heaven, and before thee. And am no more worthy to be called thy son: make me as one of thy hired servants. **Luke15: 17-19.**

In Luke 15, the prodigal son asked for his inheritance and left his father's house to go experience the world. At first, his life was good, but it all changed after some time. He ended up alone, broke, hungry, smelly, and far away from the people he loved and those that loved him. All the friends he had gained through his prodigal living were gone when he needed them the most. While he had plenty, while he had his friends, while he had his money, he was not thinking about home, but when he lost everything, he came to his senses. Sometimes rock bottom gives us the right perspective. We must take note that the son humbled himself. He recognized his error, and decided he was going to return home to his father, even wanting to be a servant. When he finally reached home, his father saw him a long way off and ran and hugged him with compassion.

Somewhere in the mixture of heartbreaks, disappointments, and wrong choices, maybe you have found yourself far away from home, far away from God. Whether it be a few steps away or a mile, God wants you to draw closer. The Lord is waiting for you to return to His loving arms. Perhaps you are ashamed and worried about what people will say if you return. Let me say this, God wants you back dirty, smelly, filthy, broken, empty, or abused. He can turn your mess into a message! It is time to come back home and take your rightful place.

Reflection

Have you strayed away from God? Circle **YES/NO.** If yes, what changed the dynamics of your relationship?

Are you ready to come back home? Circle **YES/NO.** If no, then why?

_____

_____

_____

_____

_____

_____

If yes, say this brief prayer below.

Dear Lord, I've strayed so far away from home and made some bad choices. I've been hurt and I've hurt people. Please forgive me for how I've hurt you and hurt others. I want to come back home and return to my rightful place. Create in me a clean heart oh God and renew a right spirit within me. Thank you for loving me. Thank you for another chance. Help me to Get Up from this pit and rise to my full potential and claim my rightful place in the Kingdom. Free me from thoughts of self-condemnation, guilt, and shame. Come into my heart and be my Lord and Savior once again. In Jesus' name, Amen.

4

Restoration

"But the father said to his servants, Bring forth the best robe, and put it on him; and put a ring on his hand, and shoes on his feet: And bring hither the fatted calf, and kill it; and let us eat, and be merry: For this my son was dead, and is alive again; he was lost, and is found. And they began to be merry." **Luke 15:22-24**

The meaning of the word restoration according to the Oxford dictionary on Google is, "the action of returning something to a former owner, place, or condition". Continuing the story from the previous devotion, when the son came back, he was willing to be a servant. He figured all the things he had done and all the filth he was in meant he was not worthy enough to be a son anymore.

The father expressed such joy at seeing his son return home that he didn't question what he had done, where he spent the money, or why he was back. He was just glad his son was home. When the son asked to be a hired servant, the father never even responded to him. He turned to the servants and told them to bring out some things, and each item gave insight to how his father felt about him, and how God feels about us. Each item showed the father restoring him to full sonship.

God's desire is to offer us restoration through repentance, forgiveness, and compassion. That restoration is still available to you today. Whatever you have done, God will forgive and restore you to your rightful place in Him. Stop focusing on your past mistakes when He isn't concerned about them.

The Lord is always willing to restore, heal, and love on you. He will give you beauty for your ashes. He will wipe every tear from your eye and be your comfort and peace. Will you allow Him to restore you? Will you allow Him to finish what He has started in you? Will you allow the prophecy over your life to be fulfilled by surrendering to God?

Reflection

Do you believe God wants to restore you? Circle **YES/NO.**
If no, why not?

Restoration is yours if you take the step. Are you ready?

5

Don't Look Back

"But his wife looked back from behind him and she became a pillar of salt". **Genesis 19:26 KJV**

Sodom was filled with sin and abomination, so great it reached God's nostrils. The city was going to be destroyed, but God was fulfilling His promise to Abraham by saving Lot and His family. They were given a direct command by the angel of the Lord not to look back. However, Lot's wife was still curious about what she was leaving. I believe she had become comfortable living in such a place. Why else would she look back when she was commanded not to? She was leaving Sodom, but Sodom hadn't left her.

So, you have decided to leave Sodom and return home to God. I want to encourage you to not look back. Well, until it's safe to do so, and that is, only when God says it is okay. The Lord wants to give you a new appetite for greater things, a new life, a new hope, but if you are focused on the past and what you will lose, you will run back. Don't look back even when it feels like you're losing all you've ever known. Maybe that's the exact way Lot's wife felt. Still, she had a choice to make, leave and live or stay and die.

God is saying, "My child, there's so much I desire to show you. I see that you have returned home, but don't look back and get drawn into your old desires. Follow me and I will lead you to green pastures. I will show you beauty like you've never seen and reveal mysteries to you. Keep your eyes focused on me. What you left behind was necessary so you can become the woman I have called you to be."

Reflection

Be honest when answering this question, as it will help you identify your triggers. What are the things that entice you to look back?

What are some measures you can put in place to stop going back to those things?

6

The Father's Love

"And will be a Father unto you, and ye shall be my sons and daughters, saith the Lord Almighty". **2 Corinthians 6:18 KJV**

Fathers play a very important role in the lives of sons and daughters. There's an unexplainable bond that forms and that's why when daddy isn't around, a lot of young girls and young men have an emptiness. As a young girl growing up, I did not have my father in my life. It was hard, hearing everyone boast about their father, when mine was in the wind.

I spent a lot of time searching for a father's love. I chased many relationships trying to fill that void, but to no avail. Those poor choices led to even more heartbreak. I was not respected or valued, and my self-esteem sunk even more. I thought I was all alone without my father. Even though I had other role models and male father figures, my heart longed for my dad. As I reflect on my life, I realize I had a Father with me all along. A Father who was loving, protecting, and providing. He was always there, waiting for me to accept His love and His presence in my life.

Today, I hope that you truly understand that God's love is unconditional. Often, we believe God loves us less when we mess up big time. In returning to Him, we question how He could still love us after all we have done. And that affects our ability to accept His forgiveness. I fought so hard to accept His love after I came back until one day it all hit me: my mistakes would never change how He feels about me.

Don't for one second think that He loves you any less because you've been away from Him. His love is unconditional, and He loves you despite what you have done, or where you have been.

Reflection

Do you believe God loves you? Circle **YES/NO**. If no, why are you finding it hard to believe this?

Search the Bible and find scriptures that show God's love for you.

7

Self-Forgiveness

There is therefore now no condemnation to them which are in Christ Jesus, who walk not after the flesh, but after the Spirit. **Romans 8:1**

Choosing to forgive yourself doesn't mean that you are not taking responsibility for what you have done. It means that you have acknowledged what went wrong, but you relieve yourself from the consistent guilt trip.

Forgiving yourself will happen quicker when you understand God's love and forgiveness. I struggled deeply, like many who have fallen, to forgive myself. How could I have allowed that to happen? Why didn't I do things differently? These are just some questions that constantly run through our mind when we are caught up in guilt. God brings conviction, not condemnation. So, when you realize that condemnation is ripping you apart, know immediately that it is coming from the enemy. Yes, you made the mistakes, but why hold yourself to them for the rest of your life? It is time to move on. Stop punishing and condemning yourself when God has already forgiven you.

Self-forgiveness is a hard and long journey that must not be rushed. When you forgive yourself, you will walk through those prison bars, forget the past, and move on. Do you want to be free? Well, open the door and take those chains off. Stop bringing up what God has already forgiven. Your past has nothing to do with who you are today. I want you to get up and begin your blooming process.

Reflection

Are you finding it hard to forgive yourself? Circle **YES/NO.** If yes, why?

_____

_____

_____

_____

_____

_____

_____

_____

_____

_____

_____

_____

_____

_____

You have the power to either set yourself free or remain a prisoner of the past. What will you choose and how will you go about it?

_____

_____

_____

_____

_____

_____

_____

_____

_____

_____

_____

_____

_____

I _____ choose to forgive myself.

8

A New Name

"Neither shall thy name be called any more Abram, but thy name shall be called Abraham; for a father of many nations have I made thee.". – **Genesis 17:5 KJV**

When God changes our name, it is to give us a new identity. I believe it is one of His ways to rebrand us. Our names play an intricate role in our purpose, so we must be careful what we answer to. The Lord called Abram from the land of Ur and made him some promises if he would only step out and follow Him. After some time had passed, with hiccups in-between from Abram, the Lord changed his name. Abram's name, meaning "high father," was changed to "Abraham," meaning "father of a multitude". This new name was a way to assure Abraham that God's plan would be fulfilled. God was probably reaffirming His promise to give Abraham the promised son.

When I first came to Barbados from Guyana, it was a difficult move because I was bullied and called so many names. It hurt to hear people say things like, "The best Guyanese is a dead one." This was said by both kids and adults. However, over the years, God showed me it doesn't matter what they call me.

Sis, it doesn't matter what you did; it doesn't matter your family background, it doesn't matter what areas you've failed, it doesn't matter how many sexual partners you've had. When God calls you, He gives you a new name, a new purpose, and a new identity. Today, God longs to give you a new name and new promises, but you must let Him in.

Reflection

My name means 'Resurrection' and that's God's assurance that I will get up despite the challenges of life. What does your name mean?

What are the names people have called you?

Who does God say you are?

9

Spirit vs Flesh

"But I keep under my body, and bring it into subjection…"
1 Corinthians 9:27

There is always a battle between the flesh and the spirit. When we decide to get up from our rut, that doesn't mean that the flesh won't try to rear its ugly head. Going through my process of healing and transformation, I struggled with the memories. We believe that when we say yes to God, everything will work out perfectly and we won't have to fight the enemy anymore. WRONG!

The Apostle Paul was right in saying that a man must beat his body into subjection. If you want to win the fight, then you must fight your flesh. The heart/flesh wants what it wants at all costs, but it doesn't mean you have to give in. Satan knows what you like, what you have done, and what triggers you. Therefore, he will try his best to bring up the past and ruffle your fleshly feathers to make you slip. You must gain control and not indulge in your desires. This requires a life of sacrifice. One where you decide that doing what you don't want to do is beneficial for your long-term goals. Eternity with Jesus.

Also, note that this is not something you do one day and believe you have mastered it. This will call for continuous sacrifice and submission. If you want to win the battle over your flesh, you must stay on course and fight daily. It's not a onetime fight, it's a daily war. So you have to stay prayed up and in the word of God. If you stumble, find yourself at the feet of Jesus. He's your advocate.

Reflection

List the issues of your flesh you are currently struggling with. Ask yourself if you are willfully entertaining them.

What is the plan to gain control?

10

Trauma in Traffic

*"But Esau ran to meet Jacob and embraced him, he
threw his arms around his neck and kissed him."*
Genesis 33:4 NIV

What is trauma in the traffic? I see a person's life as traffic,
consistently moving, stopping, slowing down, and at other
times moving full speed ahead. When you are trying to
move on with your life, it is likely that you will come face
to face with old trauma. This is that I call meeting trauma
in the traffic.

One night I was out having dinner with my best friend and
my sister, and I saw someone who had treated me unfairly
and spoke very belittling to me in the past. When I saw the
parked vehicle, I instantly felt a burning rage within me,
and many thoughts crossed my mind about what to do. I
messaged my friend Shannon and explained to her what
was happening and how I felt, and she gave me wise counsel.
Although my flesh was enraged, my spirit knew better and
so I did nothing as we agreed. I tried to enjoy the evening.
Still, deep down inside, I felt sad all over again.

That night, I met my old trauma in the traffic of life, and it opened my eyes and made me realize I hadn't fully healed, nor had I forgiven that person. I came home and cried my heart out to God and asked Him to help me completely forgive and let go.

The last time they had seen each other, Jacob had swindled Esau's birthright and blessing, so Jacob probably did not expect Esau to do what he did. Esau met his old trauma in traffic, but he had already forgiven his brother and moved past the situation. Therefore, his response was one of love and not of anger. We can learn from Esau here. He forgave his brother and did not allow the past to hinder his new journey.

I dare say unless you forgive, your trauma will hold you captive. It will keep you bound and stagnant. Esau did not allow that to be his story, and neither should you. What will you do when you encounter trauma in the traffic on your journey to purpose? Will you allow your flesh to rise, or will you forgive and let it go?

Reflection

What is your response to meeting your trauma in traffic?

11

Forgiveness of Others

Therefore if thou bring thy gift to the altar, and there rememberest that thy brother hath ought against thee; Leave there thy gift before the altar, and go thy way; first be reconciled to thy brother, and then come and offer thy gift". **Matthew 5:23-24 KJV**

To forgive means to pardon someone for a mistake or a debt. It's painful when others have hurt or betrayed our trust. It hurts even more when we have confided and told them what hurts us, and they do it anyway. We are filled with anger and feel betrayed. This anger festers if not dealt with, and we become bitter. What also makes us angry is people manipulating and gaslighting us. They make themselves the victim and us the perpetrator.

Is it really forgiveness if you keep bringing it back up? What if God forgives us but still brings up our past daily? Sadly, many marriages and friendships are broken and lost because of this. While a person says they forgive, it only takes an argument or a misunderstanding for the situation to be used as a grenade to win. This is not forgiveness.

I have struggled with forgiveness for many years in my life and it has taken me years to realize unforgiveness is a prison of misery, but with an open gate. What that means is that we can choose to leave that place of misery. Even though you may have every right to be angry, why would you want to stay in a place of anger? Why would you want to get wrinkles by frowning, or cause your blood pressure to be high and your heart to race abnormally? Why make yourself sick?

The Lord's prayer that many of us have been taught as kids growing up says, "And forgive us our trespasses as we forgive those who trespass against us." When we read this verse, we can see there is an order. If we want to be forgiven, we must forgive others. Holding them at ransom for an apology or for your healing will only stagnate your life and hinder the Holy Spirit from moving.

"To forgive is to set a prisoner free and discover that, the prisoner was you."- Lewis B. Smedes

Reflection

Are you harboring any unforgiveness towards anyone?

What does God say about unforgiveness?

12

Journey of Healing

"For I will restore health unto thee, and I will heal thee of thy wounds, saith the Lord..." **Jeremiah 30:17**

If you don't choose to heal, your past can become an anchor, keeping you stagnant and making you bleed on those who have a bandage for your scars. Les Brown once told a story about a man whose family was killed in a fire. He had run out of the fire and before he knew it, his family was trapped inside and died. People called him a chicken, and he identified himself as such because he never healed from that trauma.

Many of us are like this chicken man, not healing from what we did or what happened to us. You have come back to God, but if you want to move forward, you must start the journey of healing. Are you trapped in cages of regret? Are you still drowning in your tears? Are you still labeling yourself based on what happened to you? Are you unable to see that you are a victor and no longer a victim?

Healing doesn't happen in an instant. It will take time, but you must begin somewhere. The journey of a thousand steps starts with you making the first one. There will be trying and testing times. Some days you will crawl, some days you will limp, some days you will fall, some days you will run. There will be days when you will cry and feel alone, misunderstood, or forsaken. Still, whatever you do, keep moving forward.

It is time to really make peace with your past and allow the Potter to put you on the wheel to get rid of all the impurities. The Lord wants to heal you spiritually, mentally, and emotionally. You have been "barely making it" long enough.

Reflection

Is something in your past stopping your healing process? If yes, list whatever it is below.

Remember, this journey will take time, so don't be too hard on yourself. Repeat the affirmations below.

- ❖ I will cry at times, but I will not give up.

- ❖ I will fall at times, but I will not give up.

- ❖ I will stumble at times, but I will not give up.

- ❖ The journey won't always be perfect, but it is worth it.

13

The Root

Up, sanctify the people, and say, Sanctify yourselves
against to morrow: for thus saith the LORD God of
Israel, There is an accursed thing in the midst of thee,
O Israel: thou canst not stand before thine enemies,
until ye take away the accursed thing from among
you. **Joshua 7:13 KJV**

In the scripture above, Israel was being defeated and Joshua didn't know there was an accursed thing among them. After crying out to the Lord, he was shown the root issue, and later addressed it. Because he was able to deal with the root, the people of Israel regained the victory.

The first step to healing is identifying the root cause of the issue, regardless of if it was self-inflicted or done by someone else. I remember a while back there was water gushing daily on my property. As days went by, it continued to get worse, so I got concerned about the rising of my water bill and how soppy the property was becoming. Investigations were made, questions were asked and to my absolute amazement, the gushing water was coming from a house behind mine. The problem wasn't caused by me, but it was surely affecting me.

Many of you have been battling the consequences of situations you didn't create. Maybe from a parent, family member, friend, spouse, whoever. But it is still affecting you to this day. The gushing waters have swamped your life like it did my property, and possibly left you depressed and confused. Every problem you encountered was not because of what you've done, but it still needs to be addressed.

If you want to heal, then you must find the root system. What made you turn your back on God? Was it disappointment, a person, anger, fear? Knowing the cause can help you strategize and help you to not fall into the same trap again. When you recognize the root issue, a lot of your past choices will make sense. Facing the root isn't always easy as it is a scary process, but it is effective. We must never be afraid to face the dark areas of our life. Facing them is the only way to receive true healing.

Reflection

Identify the root issues in your life and make the conscious decision to deal with them.

14

Cutting Ties

As a dog returneth to his vomit, so a fool returneth to his folly. **Proverbs 26:11**

Do you find yourself returning to the same habits, lifestyle, friendships, or relationships that God delivered you from? It is easy to return to what is familiar, so it is important that you sever ties. After finding the root of the problem, make the cuts to ensure progress. Ask the Lord to show you who and what you need to sever. If you do not cut ties with some things and some people, you will end up returning to your vomit.

Have you ever deleted a photo from your gallery only to stumble onto it on your memory card or your Google drive? I recall this happening to me after thinking I had cut ties with the photos. Seeing those photos stirred up old feelings and emotions, but I was determined to get up and move forward. I did a complete clean and cut all the ties in order to move forward.

Hebrews 12 tells us to "Lay aside every weight and the sin that doth so easily beset us and run with perseverance the race set before us." Are you still attached to things you should be free of? I want to encourage you to trust God with the spiritual scissors and allow Him to cut everything that will hinder your progress. Maybe you are holding on thinking there's nothing better for you. The words God spoke in Jeremiah 29:11 are still very much relevant today. "I know the thoughts that I think towards you saith the Lord".

God knows exactly what He's doing, but our lack of trust hinders the move of God. Cutting ties will hurt, it will be painful. However, when you look back a year from now and see how God has elevated you, you will realize that the cutting was necessary.

Reflection

Make a list of the things that need to be cut off from your life.

15

Renewing your Mind

That ye put off concerning the former conversation the old man, which is corrupt according to the deceitful lusts; And be renewed in the spirit of your mind; **Ephesians 4:22-23**

The biggest battle we will fight is in our mind. Scripture tells us, "As a man thinketh so is he". If we see ourselves as defeated, then that is how we will live and view ourselves. When scripture tells us to be transformed by the renewing of our mind, it speaks of a daily process. My thoughts kept me in mental bondage and torment for a long time.

We can't renew our minds if we don't spend time in the Word which is supposed to transform us. Therefore, I struggled because I wasn't in my Bible. I eventually spent time in the Word, journaled, prayed, and pleaded with God to help me. Spiritual friends were also a great asset as they reassured me of God's power to renew and restore.

It is not God's desire or plan for you to suffer in bondage in your own mind. God wants to embrace you with His love and fill your thoughts with peace, joy, and compassion. Renewing your mind will be a consistent action of seeing things through God's lens and not through your traumatic experiences. You can walk victorious once you win the battle of the mind. Each time the thought arises, declare the Word of God over your mind, your life, and your purpose.

Reflection

What are you doing to renew your mind?

Is anything in your life being a hindrance to your growth process? Circle **YES/NO.** If yes, state what or who it is and remove them.

List the negative thought patterns and replace them with positive things.

16

Consistent Action

"The Lord our God said unto us at Horeb, you have stayed long enough at this mountain". **Deuteronomy 1:6 KJV**

The word "move" according to Oxford dictionary (Google) is defined as, "a change of place, position or to make progress". In Deuteronomy, God was ready to take the children of Israel into the land He had promised to them and their forefathers. It was time to move from Mount Horeb, and He plainly spoke to them, "ye have been here long enough and it was time for new soil." For the promise to be completed, they had to move from Mount Horeb. But they were comfortable.

When we are in a place too long, it gets cozy, and we are extremely hesitant to move. This journey of healing and growth will be one of consistent action. Where you are now is not where you will be a week, month, or year from now. The key is to move when God says to move, even when you are uncomfortable. Do not allow Horeb to be your final resting place when God is calling you higher and deeper in Him.

Sadly, we can become comfortable in our pain and trauma. Don't make that place your home. God's desire is to move you from there. If we continue to see, hear, and think through our trauma the choices we make will be tainted, and we will remain stagnant. Horeb had become familiar to the Israelites and so God needed to give them a wake-up call. Choosing to leave Horeb is recognizing that it has served its purpose, and it is okay to leave it behind. It hurts to let go, but it will kill you spiritually if you keep holding on.

Reflection

Are you comfortable in Horeb? Circle **YES/NO.** If yes, then why?

_____

_____

_____

_____

_____

_____

_____

_____

_____

_____

Moving is always uncomfortable but must be done. Will you allow God to lead you to new pastures? Circle **YES/NO**

Part 2

Things to remember when Getting Up!

17

You are Enough

"And Moses said unto the Lord, o my Lord. I am not eloquent, neither heretofore, nor since Thou hast spoken unto Thy servant: but I am slow of speech, and of a slow tongue". **Exodus 4:10 KJV**

Inadequacy is an attack of the enemy that prevents God from using us at full capacity. This mindset prevents us from understanding our true identity in Christ. It blocks us from seeing all God can do through us, because we stand in our own way.

Introspection helps us to realize that this feeling of inadequacy can come from comparing ourselves to others, word curses, generational curses, and much more. Perhaps you are wondering, "why can't I look like her?" Or maybe you are following in your parents' footsteps of being told you will never be good enough. Or is it that you were labeled the "Black Sheep" in the family?

If you believe Satan's lies, it will dampen your spirit. Therefore, when God calls you, you tell yourself, "I'm no good, I'm not worthy." Well, I'm here to tell you that you are enough. Your human limitations will make room for

God to perform heavenly expectations. Whatever you lack, God has more than enough to fill your tank. I too have had my battle with inadequacy, but the day I decided I was going to trust God was the day everything changed piece by piece.

You are not inadequate, so refuse to believe the enemy's lies. I declare every curse over your life is broken and will dry up from the root in Jesus' name. You will no longer live as a chicken; you are an eagle.

"I am not inadequate because of my lack. I'm adequate because God is my supplier." -Stacy Hyman

Reflection

Most often, feelings of inadequacy are rooted in childhood experiences. Was this the case for you?

What was said that made you feel inadequate?

How has inadequacy hindered the way you live?

What changes will you make to stomp off those feelings of inadequacy?

18

Chosen

And he said unto him, Oh my Lord, wherewith shall I save Israel? behold, my family is poor in Manasseh, and I am the least in my father's house. **Judges 8:15**

When God chose Gideon, he responded by listing reasons he shouldn't be chosen. Don't we often do this? Because of his feelings of inadequacy, he believed he wasn't the one God wanted to use. Being chosen by God has nothing to do with us and everything to do with Him. He doesn't choose us because of our political position, nationality, academic or athletic achievements, nor for our good looks. When God chooses us, He is not concerned about what we can or cannot do, because He can do all things. All He needs is an available vessel. Gideon was the least of his tribe, but God still chose him. You can see God's hand of provision and protection over his life throughout his reign. The least man became one of the greatest. Who he was born to or the little he had could not stop what God was doing in his life. Why? Because he was chosen.

God has chosen you because He knows what He can accomplish through you. Queen, straighten your crown and go forth! Don't allow anyone to disqualify you from what the Lord has called you to do. It doesn't matter what your racial, financial, or physical status is, when God calls you, He will provide and equip you with everything you need. You may be an ordinary woman in the eyes of man, but you are extraordinary to God. Others may see you as underqualified, but with God you are overqualified.

You are not too small for the space; the space is too small for you and your God. We are called and chosen by God for "Assignment" and not by "Accident". You have been carefully selected by God for His divine purpose. Do you know what that means? It means that you are more than qualified because your resume bears the seal of Jesus Christ.

Rehab was a harlot, yes you read correctly, she was a prostitute. Still, God used her to hide the spies of Israel. Also, she is in the lineage of Jesus. We often look at the physical shortcomings, when in fact, they only make room for God to do the impossible.

Reflection

Are you making excuses why God can't use you? Circle
YES/NO. If yes, then why?

Will you stop making excuses and answer the call of God? Circle **YES/NO.** Find scriptures of people who God used even though they felt incompetent. Draw strength from their stories.

19

Importance of Prayer

"Rejoice in hope, be patient in tribulation, be constant in prayer." **Romans 12:12**

Pray is a vital key to the Christian life. When we pray, we cannot see the warfare behind our prayers, all that's happening behind the scenes. Our prayers enable heaven to intervene in our earthly situations. So, if we stop praying, how will God continue to act on our behalf? Prayer gives us victory. It can move mountains and break strongholds. That's why the devil often tries to distract us. We go to pray and the phones rings or we get sleepy. Or we can't focus because our mind is filled with thoughts of the work we have to do.

God's word tells us to pray without ceasing in 1 Thessalonians 5:17. If I am being honest, at times it is hard to pray, but if we want to overcome, we cannot grow weary. When it gets harder, we shouldn't pray less, but pray harder, being assured that God will answer. Our breakthrough will come, and deliverance will arise. We must pray until something happens, until the chains are broken, until the strongholds and the strong man are bound.

This is how to upset the enemy. We push through when he wants us to quit; we fight when the pressure is unbearable, because our breakthrough will be unbelievable. Pray until something happens, don't lose hope, and don't quit. It doesn't have to be long or filled with big, extravagant words. It is a simple conversation with God. If you want to see the move of God, pray. If you desire a closer walk with God, pray.

Reflection

Is your prayer life consistent? Circle **YES/NO.** If no, then why?

If you struggle with inconsistency, make a list of the things and people below and map out a prayer structure.

20

Adhering to Wise Counsel

"But he forsook the counsel the old men gave him and consulted the young men who grew up with him and which stood before him". **1 Kings 12:8 KJV**

Who you surround yourself with and take advice from is significant. It is better to adhere to wise counsel and gain than to disobey and lose. King Rehoboam inquired of the old wise men who had counseled his father on a very delicate matter. He was given the advice not to make the people's burden any heavier, but he did not adhere. Instead, he listened to the young men who had grown up with him, and it didn't end well.

I can recall the countless times I've acted like this young king. Seeking wise counsel but still choosing to listen to my counsel or others who were just like me. This is how I strayed away from God in the first place. Today's society often pushes the agenda that the counsel of the elders is outdated and unnecessary. But they can advise because they've walked the path before. They know all the potholes on the road and only want us to avoid them. I recall reading a quote that said, "A wise man learns from his mistakes; a wiser man learns from the mistakes of others". Now that

I'm wiser and older, I realize that our elders have been trying to guide us away from the potholes they fell in and the big rocks they stumped their toes on.

It is important that you understand your decisions will have consequences. Therefore, who you listen to will determine whether you face good or bad consequences. Listen to wise counsel and gain rather than lose.

Reflection

Do you see the importance of adhering to wise counsel?
Circle **YES/NO.**

Who are you taking counsel from?

21

Build the Right Way

"Except the Lord build the house, they labour in vain that build it: except the Lord keep the city, the watchman waketh but in vain". **Psalm 127:1 KJV**

Before building, there are a few steps that must be cleared before construction can begin. The land has to be surveyed, and the relevant authorities must be given written proposals, and the builder has to wait for their approval before they build. How many of us have begun construction without God's consent? How many of us are entangled and facing consequences because we didn't verify the land before we began to build?

Should the relevant authorities become aware of an illegal structure, it is taken down immediately. In a similar manner, God wants to tear down structures that were not in His plans from the beginning. Scripture tells us that our labor is in vain if God is not our chief builder and cornerstone. I feel the shift of the Holy Spirit and I sense we are in a season where God is tearing down structures that were set up in His name, but not according to His will. How many of us are in jobs, relationships, ministries etc. that God said to walk away from?

God is about to disrupt what you thought was in order but wasn't in His order. Except God builds the house, we labor in vain. When we build our way, we build fast and on shaky ground. We are left exhausted; we feel used, abused, neglected, and rejected. Building God's way will require us to give Him total control. It's trusting the decisions He makes because He has the blueprint. Sis, the glory of the latter house shall be greater than the former. Trust God. He knows what He's doing, the best is yet to come.

Reflection

What have you built without God's approval?

Are you willing to tear down those structures and start over with Him as the foundation?

22

Hold Your Position

"If it be so, our God whom we serve is able to deliver us from the burnt fiery furnace and He will deliver us out of thine hand. But if not be it known unto thee O king that we will not serve thy gods, nor worship the golden image which thou hast set up." **Daniel 3:17-18 KJV**

It takes courage to stand up for what you believe in, especially when it is going against the tide. Boldness is needed if you don't want to compromise your beliefs and standards. As Christians, we have to hold our position and speak out in a world that will try to keep us silent. In battle, when soldiers go to war, the captain often gives the command, "Hold your position". Under no circumstances are they allowed to move or do anything unless commanded. Even in the face of death, they have to maintain their position. Similarly, as God's chosen people, we must hold our position even in the face of trials and temptations. We must stand, unwavering in our faith, suited in the full armor of God.

When it comes to an unwavering position, I am reminded of the three Hebrew boys. They would not bow down to an idol even though their lives were threatened. In the heat of a furnace that was seven times hotter, they held their position and did not compromise. Can you imagine that? They declared, "even if our God doesn't deliver us, still, we will not bow down." Face to face with death, they clung to their faith in God. They had already died to this life and did not fear death. What about you? Is your mind made up? You are called and chosen by God to do a great work, but you must hold your position at all costs.

Reflection

What is one thing that would make you think about moving from your position?

_____

_____

_____

_____

_____

Have you experienced a "hold your position" moment? If yes, what did you do?

_____

_____

_____

_____

_____

How can you prepare yourself to stand ground when faced with similar situations?

23

Take Heed

"But of the tree of the knowledge of good and evil, thou shalt not eat of it: for in the day that thou eatest thereof thou shalt surely die". **Genesis 2:17 KJV**

God commanded Adam and Eve not to eat from the tree of knowledge of good and evil. Eve, however, was subtly deceived and ate the fruit. She completely ignored what God had said. Why? Because the enemy mixed truth with his lies. Somehow, we believe Satan shows up with horns and fire breathing from his nostrils. Listen, he shows up as an angel of light. How many times were you deceived and then after asked yourself how it happened? It was because he was in camouflage.

On this journey, knowing the voice of God will be important. By knowing His voice, you will know the counterfeit when it comes. You must always pay close attention because he always mixes God's truth with his lies. Before you know it, you are trapped in sin. 1 Thessalonians 5:22-24 says, *"Abstain from all appearance of evil"* We are not to even entertain the appearance of evil. If you continue to play with fire, one day you will eventually get burned.

By taking heed, we can save ourselves from the consequences of poor choices. The psalmist David wrote in Psalm 119:105 KJV "Thy word is a lamp unto my feet and a light unto my path." If we take heed to the word and voice of God, it will save us.

Reflection

Take stock of your life and ask yourself if you are currently being deceived by something/someone masquerading as an angel of light.

What can you do to sharpen your discernment?

24

Putting away Childish Things

"When I was a Child I spake as a child I understood as a Child, I thought as a child but when I became a man, I put away childish things." **1 Corinthians13:11 KJV**

Age isn't a sign of maturity, actions are. When I was a little girl, all I thought about was sweeties and bubbles. I enjoyed running about and playing with my friends, doing things kids did. We spent countless times playing hide and seek, board and card games, and got into silly fights and quarrels. Some of us even told lies and stole here and there.

I concur with the Apostle Paul, because now that I am a woman, I had to put those childish behaviors away. I cannot waste time running about telling lies and being involved in meaningless quarrels and gossip. My actions must be wiser and carefully thought through. I realize that just because I carry double digits, doesn't mean I have double wisdom. If I don't put those childish things away, no matter what age, I will still be immature. Paul uses the growth of a child to show the progress of the Christian. We are not supposed to be at the same stage we were twenty years ago.

What I've also learned is that everyone has their own growth stages and their individual processes. No one is to be looked down upon, instead we ought to encourage, motivate and pray for them. It is important that you put away childish speaking, childish thinking, and childish reasonings. How else are you supposed to mature in Christ?

Reflection

Are you taking steps towards maturity? Circle **YES/NO.**
What childish thing haven't you put away?

What work is needed to deal with the things you have listed?

25

Always on the Watch

"Behold He that keepeth Israel neither slumber nor sleep." **Psalm 121:4 KJV**

I stand amazed at how God works on our behalf. What amazes me more is even when we don't see it or know it, He's behind the scenes working. I recall one night while cooking saying to myself, "I'll just rest for five mins." When I went to sleep, it was about 10:00pm but I jumped up around 4:00am the next day.

When I realized my error, I cried out, "My God, my God!" All I could do was thank Him for preserving me and my sister's life. This was not the first time God has spared my life like this. I recall even as a child being so enthusiastic and wanting to do as I saw granny do. I woke up early trying to cook for everyone, but fell asleep and thankfully no one was harmed, nor was there a fire.

We often doubt that God is really working things out for us when we see nothing. But if we stop to think of all the things He does behind the scenes, while we sleep, while we drive, while we work, we'd be more grateful. The Lord is always on watch and even when things go wrong; they don't take Him by surprise. Even when things go bad, He will work them out for your good. God is your lawyer, your firefighter, doctor, and high priest. He's behind the scenes, overseeing the operations of your life. He is always on watch and ready to defend and deliver, to heal and help, and to comfort. He that keepeth you will neither slumber nor sleep.

Reflection

List some scenarios that showed you God is always on the watch. Use these as reminders of His protection and thank Him for all He has done and will continue to do.

Make a gratitude list below.

26

Called for a Purpose

For if you remain completely silent at this time, relief and deliverance will arise for the Jews from another place, but you and your father's house will perish. Yet who knows whether you have come to the kingdom for such a time as this?" **Esther 14:14**

Purpose: the reason for which something is done or created or for which something exists.

God is calling you to be a woman who stands out, speaks out and who puts her life on the line for such a time as this. This is the time and season where people need to see the power of God shown forth in their lives. Esther was a perfect example of being called for a purpose. There had to be thousands of women who auditioned for the role, but the orphan Jewish girl was chosen as Queen. Note, when we are called it is to do the work of the Lord. Esther was not positioned in the palace to wear fancy clothes and host multiple parties.

When Mordecai told her what was going on behind the King's back and what she would need to do, she wasn't eager to fulfill his request. Fear of the unknown held her in its clutches. We are expected to put aside fear and do what God asks us to do. Esther's cousin told her God had carefully orchestrated her in His plan for the Jew's deliverance. She went into prayer and fasting and did the right thing. She said, "If I perish, I perish." This was her understanding that she was called for a purpose bigger than her. God moved on her behalf and the Jews were delivered.

You may say, "but God why me? Well, you are chosen because you have what it takes. People talked about Jesus and said, "Can anything good come from Nazareth?". That same Jesus paid our debt and earned us eternal life. This world needs shaking up! It's time for the queens to arise and claim their position in the Kingdom!

Reflection

What is your collective purpose in the body of Christ?

What is your individual purpose?

Are you taking the steps to fulfilling that purpose?

27

Waiting to be Commissioned

But they that wait upon the Lord shall renew their strength; they shall mount up with wings as eagles; they shall run, and not be weary; and they shall walk, and not faint. **Isaish 40:31**

Before David became king, he was just a little shepherd boy faithfully doing his duties. Little did he know God was preparing him to be king over Israel. When you are focused on the will of God, He will take care of what concerns you. Even though you have been chosen and anointed, don't run ahead of God. The period of waiting to be commissioned is needed.

The prophet Samuel saw David's brothers as qualified, but God rejected them all. God wanted David, and that was final. When David was anointed by Samuel, he still had to wait in line to be appointed as King because Saul was still reigning. What do we do when a promise has been made but not manifested? We wait until God gives us the go ahead. The Lord was preparing David. If he was going to lead God's people, he had to learn the duties of a shepherd from the Good Shepherd. David waited and waited and waited and kept serving. Can you serve faithfully as you wait upon God? *"Take care of God's business and He will take care of yours"- Cheryl Rudder*

When the time was right, God moved David from anointed to appointed king over Israel. Similarly, He is preparing you before He sends you out. You are not being overlooked; you are being prepared for what you've prayed for. As you wait in line, allow God to prepare and prune you. When it's your time, the Lord will find you, anoint you and appoint you, and you will be ready.

Reflection

Do you feel overlooked when you see others being blessed? Circle **YES/NO**. If yes, why?

_____

_____

_____

_____

_____

_____

Are you trying to rush ahead of God? Circle **YES/NO**. If yes, why?

_____

_____

_____

_____

_____

What can you do while in the waiting room to be commissioned?

28

Trust in the Lord

"Trust in the Lord with all thine heart; and lean not unto thine own understanding. In all thy ways acknowledge him, and he shall direct thy paths".
Proverbs 3:5-6 KJV

It can be scary when God calls us into the deep waters, fully submerged. However, He will not call us where He cannot provide, protect, or fulfill His purpose for us. Trust is hard, especially when you have been disappointed all your life. This can easily spill over into your relationship with God if not addressed. For example, a girl who has been disappointed repeatedly by her dad can have trust issues with God because she believes He will also let her down if she releases control and is vulnerable.

"Never be afraid to trust an unknown future to a known God" -Corrie Ten Boom.

The Lord knows what He's doing and unlike us; He knows what tomorrow holds. It's easy for us to trust God when everything is going well. When our cupboards are filled, bills are paid, and we still have a stable job with a fixed income. However, our trust is really tested when those things are taken away or lost. Job was esteemed as a perfect man, he was blameless. He lost everything through testing, but he remained faithful to God. He boldly proclaimed in Job 19:25 KJV "For I know that my redeemer lives".

Likewise, we must trust God even when the circumstances don't seem to be in our favor. Trust is a hard thing, but what do you have to lose? The Lord is always faithful, so who better than to put your trust in? Man will fail, but He never fails. I end with these words from Apostle Rudder: *"God will always give us the best."* He makes no mistakes, so don't be afraid to trust Him. Don't be afraid to hold His hands, don't be afraid to surrender completely.

Reflection

Do you trust God? Circle **YES/NO.** If no, then why?

_____

_____

_____

_____

_____

_____

_____

_____

_____

_____

_____

_____

_____

Search the bible for people that trusted in God and He came through. Use is as ammunition for when the doubt tries to creep in.

29

Delayed not Denied

"For the vision is yet for an appointed time, but at the end it shall speak, and not lie: though it tarry, wait for it; because it will surely come, it will not tarry".
Habakkuk 2:3 KJV

There are many instances I can recall where I did not receive that which I prayed or longed for. Many times the doors were closed, and I did not receive the opportunity. Did that mean God rejected me? No it didn't, but at the time I felt rejected. When faced with these circumstances, we automatically look at ourselves and think that something is wrong with us. Let me say this: what God has for you is for you!

I recall applying and doing an interview for a job I wanted. In my opinion, everything went well. I waited excitedly for a call, but it never came. I started to feel like I probably wasn't good enough, but that was a lie from the enemy. God spoke to my heart after feelings of discouragement set in. "It's not that the space is too big for you, it's that you are too big for that space", He said. I was speechless. God doesn't want us to dilute ourselves to be accepted. He doesn't want us to squeeze into places, but to have room to elevate. Don't be disheartened when you are delayed. When met with detours and setbacks, trust that God's ultimate plan for your life will come to pass.

"Though the vision tarry, wait for it". There is an appointed time for each level of your life. You are not being denied, it's just a minor setback for a major comeback. Your delay is not, "No, you can't have this". Rather it's "No, not this one or not now".

Maybe you'd like to own your own car, but you are met with delays. Seek God in prayer and listen for what He's trying to say to you. God may not be saying you can't have a car. Maybe He's saying you can't financially sustain it right now. There is always a message in a delay and with the right perspective, we will realize it's not a denial just a delay.

Reflection

Do you feel you're being denied currently? Circle **YES/NO.** If yes, what is the situation?

Despite the disappointment, how can you change your attitude?

30

Destiny over Desire

"For I am in a strait betwixt two, having a desire to depart, and to be with Christ; which is far better."
Philippians 1:23 KJV

Queen, as you embark on your journey to getting up and fulfilling your purpose, there will be many decisions to be made. As you spread your wings and fly, choose destiny over desire. Allow God to be your compass and satisfaction. Many times I was at this crossroad, having to choose between the two. Knowing that my flesh wanted to take me away from my destiny. The thing is, choosing destiny is never easy. It will bring you to your knees and to tears. Your tears, however, will wet your soil and give you such a bountiful harvest.

Remember to *"Keep thy heart with all diligence; for out of it are the issues of life"*. Proverbs 4:23 KJV. Consecrate your heart to God and let Him control your heart strings. Don't make choices without His approval. Weigh the pros and the cons. Is that thing you desire worth losing your salvation? Is it worth delaying your destiny? There's great work that only YOU can do. Perhaps all you've been doing is choosing your desire and delaying your destiny. Well, it's time to rise. It's time to dust yourself off and take up your bed up and walk boldly into your purpose. I believe in you; God believes in you, and you should too.

Reflection

What are your desires? Are they a hindrance to your destiny?

What is your destiny? What has God called you to do? What will you choose?

31

Tell your Story

"Come, see a man, which told me all things that ever I did: is not this the Christ?". **John 4:29 KJV**

After the woman at the well had an encounter with Jesus, she was filled with such excitement that she ran to tell all whom she knew to come see a man. She was saying, *"Come see a man that talked to a mere Samaritan. Come see a man who knew my sin and didn't stone me. Come see a man who gave me living water that I never have to thirst again."*

Are you telling people about the Man who changed your life? The God who forgave you and made it possible for you to get up? Everything you have been through was all a test and has led you to this place. A testimony of God's grace, forgiveness, love, provision, protection, and much more. People need to hear your testimony that they too can overcome like you have. Often, we keep quiet about what God has done in our lives. It is time for you to boldly declare the magnificent works of God.

Let your voice be heard. This is your time and season to boast about what God has done in your life. This is not the time to be timid and overwhelmed with fear. Don't stay silent and shrink back. Do not play with your anointing. You may think that your broken life couldn't possibly help someone, but it can. Your testimony may very well be someone's survival guide. Your story may be the light they need to overcome.

Reflection

What has God done for you?

Have you been telling your story? Circle **YES/NO.** If NO, what is hindering you from telling your story?

Are you ready to share your story? Start telling people about the goodness of God.

7 Steps to Getting back Up!

Take stock of your life.

What is stocktaking? "The action of reviewing and assessing one's situation and options". In like manner, we must take time to introspect our lives and take spiritual stock. As we do this, we will identify the bad choices we've made. The bad trade partners, unprofitable friends, and toxic relationships/friendships. Take some time away from everyone and journal. Remove the old unprofitable stock and make room for new stock.

Crying is therapy too!

I recall the day God gave me this revelation. Crying can often be viewed as weakness, vulnerability, or deceit and many other things. But crying helps to relieve our hearts from the burden of trauma. Jesus himself wept as scripture tells us in John 11:35 KJV.

Don't become sick trying to keep it all in. As you take stock, you will cry, so journal your honest feelings. Write exactly how you feel about the situation or person. As you do this, God will work on your heart, and healing will spring forth. Bottling our emotions is like squeezing a bottle. As the pressure increases, the bottle goes pop! God made us with emotions so it's perfectly okay to have them. However, they are not meant to control us. We can control them with the help of Jesus.

Spend time in prayer and the Word.

We overcome by the Word of God and through prayer we make our requests known unto God. Philippians 4:6-7. Many times we struggle and stay in cycles because the power of the Word is not present in our lives to bring deliverance. When Jesus was tempted by the devil, He used the Word each time. The Word of God is our defense and will deliver. Prayer is also our weapon. When we pray, demons tremble, strongholds are broken, chains are loosed and we shake the enemy's camp. Prayer gives God access to intervene in our situation. Prayer is us exalting the only One who can deliver us.

Set a certain amount of time to pray every day and you will see the transforming power of God. Make a prayer list of things and people to pray about. Even pray for those who hurt you. There have been times I prayed for my enemies to change, and instead God changed me. Prayer works.

Praise God in your storm.

Difficulties are not meant to lessen your worship but to push you to tap into God's presence even more. Matthew

26 speaks of the woman with the Alabaster box. She took the precious ointment, and she worshipped at Jesus' feet. When we face heartbreaks, we tend to listen to sad music, R&B, etc. I know all about this, my playlist was full. But I must say, these songs don't help. They will keep you trapped, bitter, angry, and stuck in the cycle of your trauma. Your breakthrough will come when you worship. As you feed your spirit the right things, you will begin to heal. In Biblical times, whenever there was a war or battle, praise would go first. Let praise go before your battles and God will give you the victory. Praise leads the way to breakthroughs and new blessings.

Keep moving forward

As you start your journey to getting back up, there will be times you will stumble. Don't let that disqualify you from the race. Remember, you have an advocate if you should sin. **1 John 2:1.** I stumbled even after I decided to get back up. I kept falling repeatedly. Many days it was my temper, lust, identity crisis, unforgiveness, sometimes it was pornography.

I kept returning to God each time and He would always forgive me, extending grace. I cried many tears, but I refused to stay down. I chose to get up and keep moving forward. Sometimes I ran, sometimes I walked and sometimes I crawled, but I never stopped moving. You shouldn't stop either. Keep moving forward sis.

Be careful what you entertain.

Remember I said I used to have a playlist full of sad music. When I stopped feeding my unhealed self what it wanted, my life changed. As I renewed my playlist, my mind renewed. Guard your gateways. Be careful what you see, hear, where you go and what you do. Declutter your mind and your life. Sin is sweet and deadly, sweet to the flesh, but deadly to our spirit. Being we are born in sin and shaped in iniquity, an appetite for what is wrong comes easy. We need the Word and the power of God to give us a new appetite. The Lord wants to give you a new appetite so that you can flourish and bring forth fruit in due season. Ask yourself, is what I'm entertaining, pushing me to my purpose or pulling me away?

Choose who you want to be.

As a young girl my mother would often say to me "Once your mind is made up, no one can change it". Unfortunately, it wasn't for anything good at the time, however God gave me a new perspective. I am now determined about who I will be. This should be the same for you, Queen. You decide who you will be and what determines you. Make a vision board for yourself and commit to becoming the best version of who God created you to be. Do not allow anyone to determine who you will be. God alone has the blueprint for your life, so trust what He says about you.

I will believe what God says about me.

I will receive what God has for me.

I will possess what God has given to me.

I will celebrate who I am becoming.

Declarations

I am ....

I will ....

I have ....

I forgive myself for ....

I forgive ....

I am proud of myself for ....

I will not ....

I refuse to ....

I will rise above ....

I will overcome ....

I will own my own ....

I am healed from ....

I am free from ....

I cut ties with ....

Made in the USA
Middletown, DE
10 March 2025

72460225R00083